What Do We Know About Dragons?

by Ben Hubbard

illustrated by Andrew Thomson

Penguin Workshop

For Barb, Heather, Nadia, and Tyler:
Canadian compadres—BH

For Rhia, Cerys, and Esme—AT

PENGUIN WORKSHOP
An imprint of Penguin Random House LLC
1745 Broadway, New York, NY 10019
penguinrandomhouse.com

Library of Congress Cataloging-in-Publication Data is available.

First published in the United States of America by Penguin Workshop, 2026

Manufactured in the United States of America
CJKW

ISBN 9798217050345 (paperback)
10 9 8 7 6 5 4 3 2

ISBN 9798217050352 (library binding)
10 9 8 7 6 5 4 3 2 1

The authorized representative in the EU for product safety and compliance is Penguin Random House Ireland, Morrison Chambers, 32 Nassau Street, Dublin D02 YH68, Ireland, https://eu-contact.penguin.ie.

Contents

What Do We Know About Dragons?

Far away in an ancient land lies a dark mountain cave. The local villagers say there is treasure in the cave, but no one dares to look for it. The cave is deep and damp and smells like dead goats. But there is something far worse inside: a dragon.

The dragon is thirty feet long with green, scaly skin and a lizard-like tail. It has four clawed feet, two bat-shaped wings, horns on its head, and ridges running down its back. It sees with eyes like a snake's, smells through an elongated snout, and tastes the air with a forked tongue. Inside its mouth are rows of crooked fangs and breath so bad it can kill a bird mid-flight.

But something far deadlier comes out of the dragon's mouth: fire. The dragon can spew a stream of fire that is hot enough to melt steel. Just one fiery blast can set an entire village alight. The thought makes the villagers quiver and quake. It has been a while since the dragon last ate. Surely, it must be getting hungry?

The dragon moved to the cave many months ago and has been terrorizing the village ever since. Every couple of weeks, the dragon crawls from its lair and takes to the skies with its massive flapping wings. It plucks goats and sheep in its claws and sometimes breathes fire over a wheat field just for fun. Then it circles back to its cave to feed. But now the dragon has eaten every animal for miles around. Are the villagers next? What can they do to avoid the danger?

Luckily, help is at hand. A hero with a sharp sword has ridden in on his horse to slay the dragon. He approaches the cave. Will he find the weak spot among the dragon's scales? Or will the beast roast him and burn down the village in revenge? As the villagers nervously watch on, the dragon starts to stir.

This tale might seem familiar to anyone who comes across a dragon in a book, movie, television show, or video game. It is a modern idea of a dragon that originates from stories told in Europe hundreds of years ago. In these stories, dragons look like monstrous lizards with huge wings, sharp fangs, and terrible claws. They spend their lives attacking people and property and are often killed by heroic knights on horseback.

But this is only one idea of what a dragon might be. Most countries around the world have their own versions. Some of these dragons are snakelike serpents without wings or feet; others are covered with feathers and have bills like birds. Other dragons look like lions, tigers, and even camels. And not all of these dragons are dangerous and destructive. In many places, dragons are considered to be friendly and helpful and to bring good luck. There are probably as many different dragons as there are countries in the world.

Because there are many different dragons, there are also a lot of unanswered questions about them: Are there any photos of dragons? Has a live dragon ever been found in the wild? Have the remains of a dragon ever been dug up from deep underground? If not, then what do we really know about dragons?

CHAPTER 1
Dragons of the Ancient World

Stories about dragons are thousands of years old. We know this because dragons appear in some of the oldest human texts. Around 4000 BCE in ancient Mesopotamia (modern Iraq, Syria, and southern Turkey), people invented an early form of writing called cuneiform. Cuneiform was written on clay tablets, usually to keep records of daily life. But one day, someone in the Mesopotamian city of Sumer wrote a strange word on a tablet: *Ušumgal* (say: OO-som-garl), or dragon.

Mushussu on the Ishtar Gate

The Sumerians believed that Ušumgal was a large-jawed, desert-dwelling dragon that could only be defeated by a great warrior. But it was not the only dragon. In the nearby city of Babylon, people worshipped a dragon called Mushussu (say: moosh-U-su), which means “fierce snake.” Mushussu had a long tail, clawed feet, and a body that was part snake and part eagle. Images of the dragon adorned the city’s famous Ishtar Gate.

Other dragons appeared in Mesopotamian myths—stories told by ancient people to explain how the world was created and why certain things happen. One such Mesopotamian myth, written on clay tablets, is about the first beings: Tiamat and Apsu. Tiamat and Apsu had many children. But the children seized control and killed Apsu. This made Tiamat so angry that she transformed herself into a terrifying dragon. Her body became snakelike and covered in scales, with four clawed feet, a long neck, and a horned head. Tiamat set out to destroy everything. Only the warrior god Marduk could stop her. Marduk threw a net over Tiamat and then killed her by firing an arrow into her heart.

Marduk then formed Earth from Tiamat's body, with Babylon at its center. This, the Babylonians believed, was how the world began.

Around this time, another ancient culture was developing nearby: Egypt. Like the Mesopotamians, the Egyptians also had myths featuring dragons. Their most famous dragon was an evil monster called Apep. Apep was a cross between a snake and a crocodile and fought against the sun god Ra every day. The reddening of the sky at night was said to mean Ra had once again beaten Apep in battle.

A famous traveler to ancient Egypt was the Greek historian Herodotus (say: he-ROD-o-tus). When Herodotus visited Egypt in 454 BCE, he was shown the bones of large creatures. He was told they were dragon bones. This did not

Herodotus

surprise Herodotus—after all, there were plenty of dragons in Greek mythology. The word *dragon* even comes from the ancient Greek "drakon," which means *serpent* (a scaly, limbless reptile).

In one famous Greek myth, the hero Cadmus follows a cow deep into a forest. There he hears hissing from a cave, and a dragon emerges. The dragon is a massive, wingless serpent that spits poison from its forked tongue. It rises up above the trees like a coiled cobra and then strikes, tearing Cadmus's men apart with its venomous fangs. The dragon darts forward to bite Cadmus, but its fangs bounce off his shield. Finally, Cadmus thrusts his spear into the dragon's throat and kills it. Cadmus then builds the city of Thebes in the place where the dragon died. He even plants the dragon's teeth like seeds, and suddenly an army of soldiers springs up from the ground.

Many Greek myths were inherited by the Roman Empire, which rose to power after Greece declined. Both civilizations shared the mythical story of Medusa, a female monster with snakes for hair. The hero Perseus kills Medusa by cutting off her head, but blood from her neck soaks into the ground and gives birth to venomous winged dragons big enough to hunt elephants. Perseus then uses Medusa's head to turn a sea monster to stone and rescue the North African princess Andromeda.

Medusa

Heracles and the Hydra

Heracles was a Greek mythological hero known as Hercules by the Romans. From birth, Heracles battled serpents and dragons. As an infant in his crib, he strangled two serpents that had been sent to kill him by the goddess Hera.

As an adult, Heracles battled the Hydra: a dragon-type monster with twelve heads. This was a difficult task because every time one head was cut off, two new ones grew back in its place. With his nephew Iolaus's help, Heracles used fire to prevent the heads from growing back and finally slayed the Hydra.

Stories about dragons were one thing, but in 256 BCE, myth seemed to merge with reality. Roman soldiers in North Africa reported fighting an actual dragon. According to the poet Silius Italicus, Roman legionaries (elite soldiers) encountered the dragon by the river Bagradas in Libya. The dragon was a black muscular serpent that lived in a foul-smelling hole by the riverbank and only emerged to feed on lions and cattle who came to the river to drink water.

Now the ground shook as the dragon wriggled out of its hole and fell upon the soldiers. It coiled its body around several legionaries to crush them to death. And it tore others apart with its fangs. The remaining soldiers pulled back in terror. But their commander Marcus Atilius Regulus urged the men to attack, and with spears and arrows the dragon was slain.

The story of the dragon of Bagradas had a lasting impact. Roman historians claimed that soldiers brought back the dragon's remains to display in the city of Rome. The dragon's jawbone alone was said to be 120 feet long. Apparently, dragons were no longer simply beasts from stories but real animals found on Earth.

This was confirmed in an encyclopedia called *Natural History* by Roman senator Pliny the Elder. In the book, Pliny said that dragons came from India and often preyed on elephants. The dragons dropped onto the elephants from trees and then tried to squeeze them to death. However, this often meant the elephant collapsed, which crushed both animals to death in the process. Pliny added that if a dragon's head was cut off while it was still alive, its brain would turn into a large white gemstone called a dracontia.

The ancient Greek philosopher Apollonius of Tyana also wrote about gemstones in dragon skulls. After traveling through India in the first century CE, Apollonius wrote: "Dragons of enormous size and variety infest northern India."

As proof, Apollonius said that dragon skulls were often displayed in public and that the local people dug up dragon skulls to retrieve the gemstones inside them.

Pliny's and Apollonius's texts were widely read for many centuries. This helped spread the idea that dragons were dangerous beasts that needed to be killed. But what did the people in India, the birthplace of dragons, according to Pliny, think about them? It may have been a surprise to him that people in India and other parts of Asia had very different ideas about dragons.

CHAPTER 2
Dragons in Asia

The ancient writers Apollonius and Pliny described dragons in India as dangerous elephant killers. Did the people of India agree? There were certainly dragons in the country's own myths. These were called nagas: magical, snakelike animals with human heads. Nagas lived in vast underground palaces, where they guarded hoards of treasure. They were powerful and sometimes dangerous, but also often helped humans.

India was not the only Asian country with helpful dragons—China had them, too. Dragon worship in China is very old. A dragon statue discovered in 1987 dates to between five thousand and seven thousand years ago. This makes Chinese dragon beliefs at least as old as those of ancient Mesopotamia and Egypt.

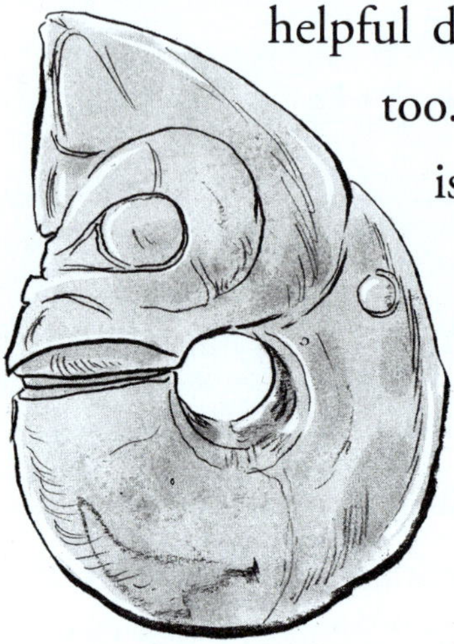

Dragon statue discovered in 1987

In ancient Chinese texts, dragons were seen as magical beings that could help humans, but they were also treated as members of the natural world. Writers described dragons as one of the 369 animal species known at that time, alongside lizards and snakes.

According to Chinese mythology, there are four main types of dragons, called longs. These longs are the Celestial Dragon (Tianlong), which guards the stars; the Earth Dragon (Dilong), which controls the waterways; the Spiritual Dragon (Shenlong), which controls the wind and rain; and a Dragon of Hidden Treasure (Fuzanglong). However, whatever the type, all longs share the same physical features, according to scholar Li Shizhen. Every long has the head of a camel, ears of a cow, eyes of a demon, neck of a snake, belly of a clam, feet of a tiger, and claws of an eagle. A long also has antler-type horns like a deer and 117 shiny scales covering its body. The dragon takes its power from a pearl that sits hidden under the folds of its chin. Longs can make fire, but this fire

can be extinguished by fire made by humans.

Longs live for many years and develop as they grow. A baby long hatches from an egg and has the body of a water snake for its first five hundred years. It then develops a tail, four legs, the head and scales of a carp (a type of fish), and a face and beard. After another five hundred years, the long grows horns, and then, five hundred years later,

it becomes a winged adult. Longs are believed to have power over water and rainfall. They also love swallows (a type of bird) and hate iron. Li Shizhen therefore suggests that people who have eaten swallows should avoid crossing water in case it rises suddenly. Those people who want water to subside can bring this about by holding a piece of iron.

Li Shizhen

As well as helping with water, dragons are also believed to cure illness. Chinese naturalists suggest that medicine made from dragon bones can treat everything from madness to diarrhea. One recipe recommends cooking the bones in hot water and grinding them into a fine powder. The powder should then be put into a gauze bag and placed inside the empty carcass of a swallow. After hanging the stuffed swallow body over a well overnight, the powder is ready to be mixed into a medicine and eaten. This medicine is meant to have divine power (like that from a god).

Because Chinese dragons were seen as divine, they became a symbol of strength. Emperor of the Han dynasty Liu Bang (206–195 BCE) told his subjects that his father was a dragon. From then on, the dragon became the emperor's symbol. Every subsequent Chinese emperor was called "the true Dragon as the Son of Heaven" and sat on the royal Dragon Throne.

Emperor Liu Bang

It later became law that only members of the royal family could wear the dragon symbol on their clothes.

Similar versions of the Chinese long were shared by other Asian countries, including Vietnam, Korea, and Japan. Korean dragons were depicted with long beards and were believed to live in rivers and lakes. They had the power to bring rain to a farmer's crops. In Vietnam, a dragon was said to have spat out the monumental limestone islands of Ha Long Bay. In Japanese

mythology, dragons could speak, change into human form, and often lived in palaces.

In one Japanese myth, a dragon hires a samurai warrior to slay his enemy, a giant centipede. The warrior's reward is a bag of rice that can never be emptied. Dragon symbols were commonly used on Japanese samurai armor and weaponry. But Japanese dragon myths were not always about warriors or weapons. A famous example is "The Fisherman and the Dragon Princess," a story about a bighearted fisherman named Urashima Taro.

One day, Urashima was walking along the beach when he saw a group of excited children. They were tormenting a large sea turtle by hammering on its shell and stopping it from returning to the sea. Urashima gave the boys some

coins to set it free. The sea turtle then swam out of sight toward the setting sun. The next day in his fishing boat, Urashima heard a voice calling his name: It was the sea turtle he had saved.

The sea turtle took Urashima to the Dragon King's palace under the sea. When they got there, the sea turtle turned into a beautiful dragon princess—this was who Urashima had saved!

The pair lived in the palace for many happy years, but Urashima missed his parents and told the princess he must return home. Before Urashima departed, the princess gave him a small box—but told him never to open it and said he must obey her words. Urashima traveled back to his village but found he had been away for three hundred years. Everyone he knew had died. Urashima sat on the shore weeping.

Borneo Dragons

The Kayan and Kenyah people of Borneo (an island in Southeast Asia) believe in dragons that bring good luck, similar to the Indian nagas and Chinese longs. The Borneo goddess of the underworld is thought to be a dragon who can control water, thunder, and lightning and who protects the living and guards the dead. Some people in Borneo say that a dragon sits on the island's Mount Kinabalu, where it guards a precious jewel. People on the island often carve images of crouching dragons into the rafters of their houses for luck.

As he had lost everything else, Urashima decided to open the princess's box. Three small purple clouds emerged and drifted over Urashima. He then began aging rapidly, and within minutes, he died.

The dragon story was supposed to teach children to not be disobedient, as Urashima had been. It also showed that Asian dragons could be pleasant and kind, unlike the scary dragons from Mesopotamia, Egypt, and Europe. However, during the Middle Ages, in European tales, dragons became even more dangerous and deadly than ever before.

CHAPTER 3
A Middle Age Tail

European dragons in the Middle Ages were big, bad, and determined to destroy. (The Middle Ages—also called the medieval period—lasted for about one thousand years from 500 to 1500 CE.) Dragons appeared in poetry, books, and illustrated encyclopedias.

However, much of the information from these encyclopedias had simply been copied from ancient Greek and Roman writers such as Herodotus, Apollonius, and Pliny. Their stories about dragons in North Africa inspired one of the most famous dragon tales of the Middle Ages: "Saint George and the Dragon."

George was probably a real Roman soldier who lived around 300 CE. However, the legend of George and the dragon only became known from the sixth century onward. According to the story, George was asked to save a Libyan king's daughter by slaying a local dragon. The king's subjects had been feeding the dragon their farm animals—and their own children when the animals ran out. The king's daughter was now next in line to be eaten. But just in the nick of time, George rode in, promptly speared the dragon, and cut off its head. George then told the king and his subjects to convert to Christianity, which they did. For his heroic deed, George was made a saint. He even became the patron saint of England.

The story of George and the dragon was probably based on the ancient Greek myth of Perseus saving Andromeda and updated for European Christian audiences of the Middle Ages.

It led to an explosion of European tales featuring dragons and heroic dragon slayers. The dragons in these tales included wingless, legless serpents known as lindworms and wyrms. There were also the more common fire-breathing, winged dragons with legs, called firedrakes, and wyverns.

Lindworm

A giant wyvern is the foe in the famous eighth-century Old English poem about the Scandinavian hero Beowulf. Beowulf is the warrior hero hired to slay a swamp monster named Grendel. Afterward, Beowulf is made king and lives happily for fifty years. But one of his subjects steals a treasure from the lair (a place where a wild animal lives) of a sleeping dragon, which then sets out for revenge. The dragon flies over Beowulf's kingdom, setting farms and villages ablaze with its fiery breath. The aging Beowulf confronts the dragon at its cave, but his men run away in fright when it spews fire at them. Beowulf is partially protected from the flames by his metal shield, but his hair is set on fire and his face is badly blistered. Beowulf tries to stab the dragon, but his sword bounces off its scales and shatters. Then a warrior named Wiglaf steps forward to help his king. But as Beowulf grabs for his dagger, the dragon darts forward and bites him in the neck with its venomous fangs.

Wiglaf stabs the dragon in a gap between its scales. As the dragon writhes on the ground, both men attack it until it is finally dead. But it is too late for Beowulf, who dies from the dragon's venom.

Beowulf is only one dragon story set in Scandinavia. The Vikings, who attacked parts of Europe between the eighth and eleventh centuries (the 700s to the 1000s), believed in many mythological dragons. According to the Viking creation myth, several dragons lived in a tree that grew at the center of their universe. Another dragon, called the Midgard Serpent, was believed to have killed the god Thor during the battle of Ragnarök, which ended the world.

In another Viking myth, a greedy dwarf named Fafnir is turned into a dragon. Fafnir's brother Regin then convinces the hero Sigurd to slay the dragon so he can claim its treasure. Sigurd does this by digging a pit in the ground and climbing into it so he can stab the dragon from below when it slithers up the path to its den.

The Vikings used the dragon as a symbol to

strike terror into their enemies' hearts. They would carve dragons as figureheads on their longships and attack monasteries and villages across Europe. The country that suffered the most from Viking attacks was England, which had many of its own tales about dragons.

Some of these English dragon stories appeared in the twelfth century's *History of the Kings of Britain*, written by Geoffrey of Monmouth. They include tales about the legendary King Arthur, his wizard Merlin, and the Knights of the Round Table. (A knight was a soldier, often on horseback and wearing armor, who served a British lord.) Like Saint George, Arthur's knights Lancelot and Gawain are still famous today as classic English dragon-slaying knights in armor.

Another famous legendary knight was John Lambton, who was said to battle against a wyrm to save his kingdom. In *The Lambton Worm*, John is the heir to Lambton Castle. He goes fishing one day instead of attending church but only catches a small eel. He throws the eel into a well and then rides away from his home, searching for adventure. Meanwhile, the eel grows into a terrible dragon, which outgrows the well and coils itself around the hill below it. The dragon eats many farm animals and several knights who try to kill it. After seven years, John Lambton returns home and finds the dragon has taken over. A wise woman tells John to wear a suit of armor covered in spikes to fight the dragon. But John must vow to then kill the first living thing he encounters after slaying the dragon, or his family will be cursed. John agrees to this and rides to face the dragon. The dragon immediately coils around John to squeeze him to death,

but in the process it cuts itself to pieces on his spiked armor. John then rides home, but his father forgets about John's promise and rides out to congratulate him. John cannot bring himself to kill his father—the first living person he encounters—and so the Lambton family is cursed forever.

Wyrms and firedrakes also feature in dragon stories from Switzerland. In one 1421 story, a flying dragon crashes into a farmer named Stempflin on Mount Pilatus, making him faint with fright.

When Stempflin wakes, he finds the dragon has left a large gemstone behind. In neighboring Austria, a dragon was said to live in the Drachenhöhle (Dragon's Cave) in Mixnitz, Styria. The dragon had eaten many of a local farmer's cattle and even a shepherd boy as well. The farmer's son decided to kill the dragon by burying a number of knives and sharp farming tools in the path the dragon took to drink. When the dragon slithered back to its den, it cut itself to pieces.

In the nearby Austrian town of Klagenfurt, another dragon was also said to be feeding on farm animals. Eventually, a team of knights hunted the dragon down and cut off its head. In 1335, the skull of this dragon was displayed in the local town hall. The skull proved to many locals that dragons really existed. In 1582, the skull was even used as a model to make a statue of the dragon, which still stands in Klagenfurt today.

The people of Klagenfurt were not the only Europeans to believe in the existence of dragons. New texts published in the sixteenth century also suggested that dragons were real. A 1587 volume of Swiss naturalist Conrad Gessner's encyclopedia included dragons among the other known animal species on Earth. Books with similar ideas soon followed.

In 1608, English author Edward Topsell wrote a book called *The History of Four-Footed Beasts and Serpents*. Topsell said the book would satisfy anybody that there were "dragons and winged serpents in the world." In the book, he claimed that apples give dragons gas, and they eat lettuce to make themselves feel better.

But Topsell was not the only author writing about dragons. Italian naturalist Ulisse Aldrovandi's *History of Serpents and Dragons*, written in 1640, discussed dragons and included drawings of them. But today it is obvious that some of these drawings are made from combining different animal parts, such as seahorses, fish, and pigs. Others also had the idea of drawing dragons by borrowing body parts from other animals. In 1696, Dutch engineer Cornelius Meyer published an engraving (an art print made by using a metal plate) of a dragon skeleton he said he discovered near Rome. However, Meyer's "dragon" turned out to have the skull of a dog, the legs of a bear, and the ribs of a fish. The dragon was clearly made up.

As time went on, science began to replace mythical beliefs about dragons with factual information. It would shine a new light on our knowledge of these animals and the stories that were made up about them.

Knuk's Dragon

Kraków is a city in southern Poland originally founded on Wawel Hill. The castle of King Krak was built on top of the hill, and below it lay the lair of a dragon. Krak had to feed the dragon farm animals to stop it from attacking—but after a while he ran out of animals.

A clever young shoemaker named Skuba decided to outsmart the dragon. He stuffed a sheep's body with pieces of burning sulfur, a poisonous chemical. When the dragon devoured the sheep, its throat began to burn. The dragon rushed to drink from the river. But water cannot extinguish burning sulfur, and so the dragon's head exploded.

CHAPTER 4
American Dragons

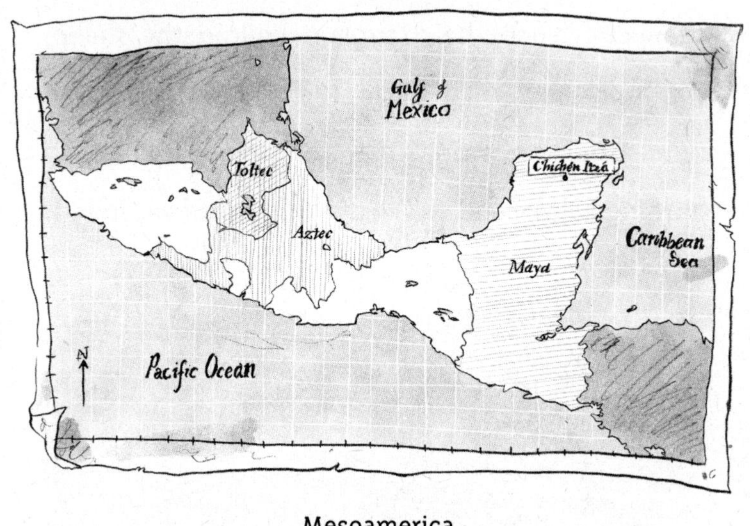

Mesoamerica

Far from Europe, the people of the Americas believed in completely different dragons. For thousands of years, cultures such as the Maya, Toltec, and Aztec lived in the region called Mesoamerica, between what are now Costa Rica and Mexico. Between 500 BCE and 900 CE, the Maya built over forty cities in modern-day Mexico, Guatemala, and Belize. These cities included Chichén Itzá, in Mexico's Yucatán Peninsula. Here, the Maya worshipped a feathered serpent called Kukulcán (say: KOO-kool-kan). Kukulcán was believed to be responsible for the wind, water, and rain. An image of Kukulcán was carved into the limestone stairway of Chichén Itzá's El Castillo. At certain times of year, the sun falls on the serpent carving, making it look as if it is slithering down the stairs.

Kukulcán carving at the Chichén Itzá temple

Kukulcán was worshipped under the name Quetzalcóatl (say: ket-sel-KOL-at) by the Toltec and Aztec civilizations that thrived farther inland from the Maya. Quetzalcóatl was a cross between a large serpent and the quetzal, a green local bird. Like Kukulcán, Quetzalcóatl was believed to have power over water, but also the stars, the sun, and in some cases, human sacrifice.

Quetzalcóatl often starred in myths alongside Tezcatlipoca (say: TESS-kat-le-poke-ah), the god of trickery and darkness. In their final encounter, Tezcatlipoca destroyed the Toltec city of Tollan and then hunted Quetzalcóatl down. During the chase, Tezcatlipoca stole all of Quetzalcóatl's powers and treasures and forced him to escape to sea by raft. However, Aztec mythology said that

Quetzalcóatl would return one day.

Some think the Aztecs believed the arrival of the light-skinned, bearded Spanish men in 1519 was actually Quetzalcóatl returning home to Mesoamerica. Unfortunately, this was not the case. Instead, the Spanish invaded, bringing violence and disease, and eventually wiping out most of the Aztec people in the process.

Inca Dragons

Between 1438 and 1533, the Inca created an empire in South America that stretched for over 2,500 miles between modern-day Peru and Chile. The Incan people worshipped a large double-headed serpent called Amaru that lived at the bottom of rivers and lakes. They believed that the dragon protected them and controlled their water. Like the Native cultures of Mesoamerica, the Inca were invaded by the Spanish in the sixteenth century. But some of their textiles, pottery, sculpture, and artworks depicting the Inca dragon survived.

Farther north, in today's United States and Canada, Native Americans and First Nations people also believed in dragon-type gods. A giant horned serpent with a crystal on its forehead was worshipped by the Cherokee. Its name was Uktena. According to myths, the crystal dazzled and confused warriors who came to kill Uktena. In these stories they usually ended up being eaten by the beast.

Another North American dragon became famous because of a painting on a cliff face in Alton, Illinois. French explorer Jacques Marquette saw the image in 1673 while traveling down the Mississippi River. Marquette said there were two of the dragons in the picture, which looked "as large as a calf; they have horns on their heads like those of a deer, a horrible look, red eyes, a beard like a tiger's, a face somewhat like a man's, a body covered with scales, and so long a tail that winds all around the body."

Marquette had discovered the Piasa, a dragon worshipped by the local Illini. In 1836, Alton professor John Russell published an article about the exact Piasa shown in the painting. He said the dragon had once terrorized the local village and eaten many humans. Warriors shot the Piasa down using poisoned arrows and then found thousands of human bones littering the Piasa's cave.

However, Russell's story took a twist when he later admitted to making it up. Sadly, the Piasa painting was destroyed to make way for a quarry and its significance may never be understood. The Piasa still appears today on tourist souvenirs in Illinois.

Russell's story was not the only time dragons appeared in nineteenth-century American newspapers. In 1882, California's *Gridley Herald* reported a story of a dragon swooping down on two lumberjacks near Hurleton, California. The men, Thomas Campbell and John Howard, said that one Friday afternoon they were startled by what looked like a flying crocodile flapping its wings forty feet above them. They said the dragon was eighteen feet long, had six wings, and had a long snout. The men shot at the dragon, which they said "uttered a cry similar to that of a calf and bear combined, but gave no sign of being inconvenienced or injured."

The bullets bouncing off the animal's body made a sound like "sheet iron," the men added. It is not known what happened to the dragon.

Another dragon report followed in another California newspaper, the *Tombstone Epitaph*, in 1890. The article said that two cowboys riding between the Huachuca and Whetstone mountains had seen a "winged monster resembling a huge alligator with an extremely elongated tail and an immense pair of wings." The men chased the creature on horseback and found it could only fly for short distances. The dragon then attacked the men, and they shot it dead.

The men examined the dragon's body and said it was 160 feet long with a wingspan of 78 feet! It also had two legs, a thick head, and eyes the size of dinner plates. The wings and body were covered with smooth black skin, which the men cut a sample of. They then rode into town. Plans were made to collect the dragon's corpse and take it to a museum, but nothing more was ever heard or reported about the matter.

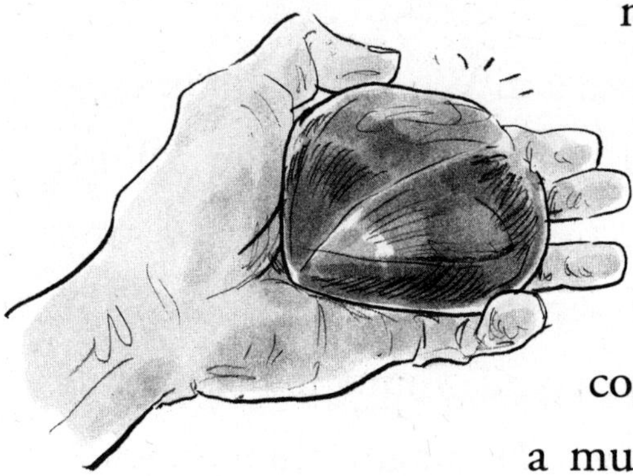

Without a body, bones, or other evidence, it was impossible to verify these newspaper articles. But over the next few decades, proof that dragons existed seemed to emerge. The bones of massive creatures were being dug up across North America, Europe, and Asia. Were these bones proof that dragons existed?

CHAPTER 5
Digging Up Dragons

In the nineteenth century, digging for ancient bones became big business. This was a time of great scientific progress, and people wanted to understand the animals that had once roamed the earth. In 1822, a new science called paleontology emerged. Paleontologists examined the remains of long-dead animals. These remains are often called bones, but they are actually fossils. A fossil is like the imprint of an animal that died long ago. Over time, its bones erode away and small stones, sand, and minerals replace them to form a rock-hard fossil.

The fossilized bones that nineteenth-century paleontologists discovered were often large and terrifying. They belonged to creatures with powerful jaws, teeth like steak knives, clawed limbs, and horned heads. This was also how many ancient texts had described dragons. Did these bones belong to dragons?

In 1830, Scottish paleontologist Hugh Falconer decided to try to answer this question. He started a search for dragon bones in India. He followed the trail of the ancient Greek Apollonius, who had reported that northern India was full of dragons and dragon skulls containing gemstones.

Falconer began digging in India's Siwalik Hills and quickly found many fossilized bones. He collected over six hundred bones in just six hours!

Some of the bones clearly belonged to a type of elephant—the prey of dragons, according to ancient stories. Other bones were more difficult to identify, but some did contain sparkling crystals. Falconer shipped five tons of bones to museums in England. Maybe closer examination would reveal what they belonged to? Some did turn out to be reptiles, such as crocodiles and tortoises. But Falconer could not identify any bones that came from a dragon.

Another country that had reported the existence of dragon bones was China. In 1919, Swedish geologist Johan Andersson and Austrian paleontologist Otto Zdansky traveled to northern China to search for themselves. They immediately found that Chinese miners had been digging up fossils for centuries before them. The miners had even washed and labeled the bones. The bones notably included the deer-type antlers that supposedly grew on Chinese dragons.

But then there was an unexpected twist. The Chinese miners told Andersson and Zdansky that all animal remains dug up from the ground were called "dragon bones" for simplicity. This information was a big deal—it meant the remains so long referred to as dragon bones in China could actually belong to any kind of dead animal. In 1842, English paleontologist Richard Owen had given a new name to the ancient creatures being discovered in large numbers by paleontologists: dinosaurs. Could many of the Chinese dragon bones therefore simply be dinosaur bones?

In 1922, American adventurer Roy Chapman Andrews decided to find out more. With help from the American Museum of Natural History, Andrews began a dig in Asia's Gobi Desert. Andrews was specifically looking for the dragon teeth and bones he had read about. The desert turned out to contain great riches for paleontologists. Andrews was amazed to find fossilized bones "strewn over the surface almost as thickly as stones." In one week, Andrews collected more than one ton of bones.

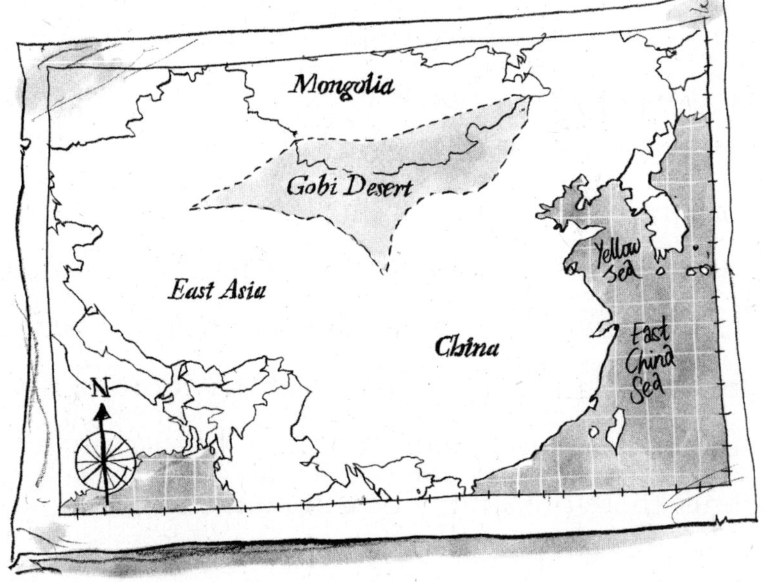

The bones of one animal found by Andrews in the Gobi Desert had many dragon features: a large jaw, four feet, and a horned head. It looked like a dragon skeleton! However, it actually belonged to a dinosaur Andrews named *Protoceratops andrewsi* (say: PRO-toe-SER-ah-tops an-DROO-zie), which had died out seventy-one million years ago.

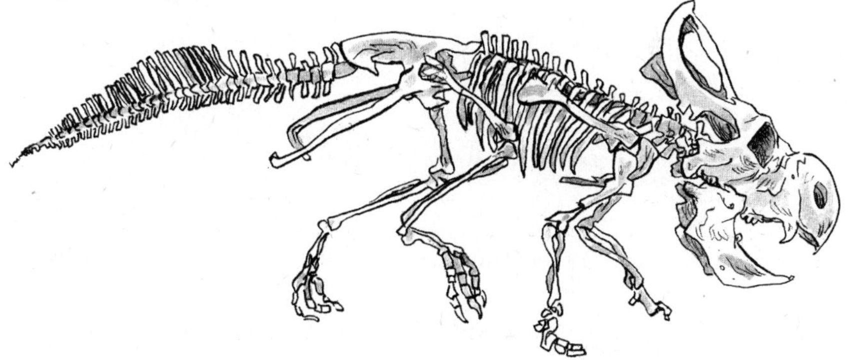

Protoceratops andrewsi skeleton

This showed how easy it was to misidentify the bones of dead animals. It also seemed that Asia would not reveal any actual dragon remains. Would paleontologists have better luck in Europe?

Roy Chapman Andrews (1884–1960)

Roy Chapman Andrews was an American explorer and adventurer who became famous in the 1920s for digging up fossils in Asia. Born in Beloit, Wisconsin, Andrews began his career in New York City sweeping floors in the American Museum of Natural History before eventually becoming one of the museum's naturalists and later its director.

He led expeditions to the East Indies and Korea and collected whale bones in Alaska before studying dinosaur remains in central Asia. Among his many finds were the first discovery of fossilized dinosaur eggs, the first *Oviraptor*, and the first *Protoceratops*.

For his pioneering paleontology, Andrews was celebrated in *Time* magazine and described his trailblazing career in several autobiographies. He is remembered today as the real-life Indiana Jones—the inspiration for the movie character played by Harrison Ford.

One place paleontologists searched was the Dragon Cave in Mixnitz, Austria, where a farmer's son had supposedly slain a dragon during the Middle Ages. Sure enough, in 1918, a number of bones were found in the cave. They turned out not to belong to a dragon but to a large prehistoric cave bear called *Ursus spelaeus* (say: ER-suss SPEY-lay-uss). This discovery led to a new theory about dragons, however. Austrian paleontologist Othenio Abel suggested that the discovery of cave bear skulls in Mixnitz during the Middle Ages may have given rise to tales about dragons living there.

Connections were being made between ancient history and medieval folklore.

The theory seemed plausible. The skulls of dead animals could easily be mistaken for dragons. This exact thing had happened in Klagenfurt, Austria, in 1335. The skull of the dragon supposedly killed by knights in armor was put on display in the town hall. It was taken as proof that dragons existed. But when the skull was examined in the modern age, it was found to belong to a woolly mammoth, a type of prehistoric elephant. The Klagenfurt skull was not a dragon but simply a case of mistaken identity.

Neighboring Switzerland had its own stories about dragons, including the dragon that flew into a farmer on Mount Pilatus in 1421. Paleontologists searching around the mountain discovered it was littered with the fossils of flying reptiles called pterodactyls (say: TERR-o-dak-tills). Pterodactyls were like large bats, with clawed feet and long jaws. Pterodactyls became extinct millions of years ago, but a pterodactyl skeleton could easily be mistaken for the remains of a dragon.

A theme was beginning to emerge. Paleontology was a new science in the nineteenth century, but people had been digging up bones since the beginning of human history. However, they were not scientists. Today we can carbon-date fossilized bones and identify the animal they came from.

Some we know are dinosaurs and flying reptiles that are millions of years old. Others, such as cave bears and woolly mammoths, are only tens of thousands of years old. But ancient humans who found these bones could not have known any of this. They must have imagined strange, monstrous creatures with terrible teeth, claws, and horns. For them, the answer was simple: They had found the remains of long-dead dragons.

But what of the dragons in India, which ate elephants and had gemstones in their skulls?

Scientists discovered that the "gemstones" found in fossilized bones were actually calcite crystals, which can form naturally over many years. The elephant bones discovered in India were found to belong to the same prehistoric animal family as woolly mammoths. Because other bones were jumbled up with these animals, people assumed they were the remains of elephants and dragons that had killed each other in battle and become entwined in death.

Even the Egyptian dragon bones seen by Herodotus in 454 BCE were later explained. In 1912, a new type of dinosaur, called *Spinosaurus*, was discovered in North Africa. *Spinosaurus* was the largest carnivore that ever lived: It had a long jaw, two feet, two clawed hands, and a large back crest that could be mistaken for wings. *Spinosaurus* was a terrifying monster by anyone's standards. But it was not a dragon.

In the end, the paleontologists of the nineteenth century did not locate any real dragon bones. But while they searched, there was an explosion in books about dragons. The modern boom of dragons in popular culture was about to begin.

The Komodo Dragon

The Komodo dragon is a large land lizard that lives on Indonesia's Lesser Sunda Islands. It can weigh three hundred pounds, has scaly skin, has a powerful tail, and is a ferocious predator. It hunts large prey such as deer and water buffalo by biting them with its serrated teeth. This causes a large wound that quickly becomes infected with the lizard's venomous saliva. The prey tries to escape but soon dies from blood loss. The dragon then tracks the dead body down with its powerful sense of smell.

The Komodo dragon is not a real dragon. It was given that name by American W. Douglas Burden, who went to Indonesia to research the lizards in 1926 and named them after the island of Komodo. Burden was an adventurer and naturalist. He wrote books about his expeditions and studies, which included both sharks and Komodo dragons. Because the lizards had not been seen by people outside Indonesia until the early part of the twentieth century, they are not connected to the dragon stories of the Middle Ages.

CHAPTER 6
Dragons in Popular Culture

While paleontologists searched around the world for dragon bones, dragon characters became the stars of children's fiction. The dragons in these books often looked like fire-breathing monsters, but some were friendly and helpful. It was as if the appearance of dangerous European dragons had been mixed with the kind personalities of Asian dragons.

A famous example is *The Reluctant Dragon* by Kenneth Grahame. The 1898 story is a twist on the tale of "Saint George and the Dragon." In the book, a young boy meets a gentle, poetry-loving dragon. But the local townspeople find out about the dragon and hire Saint George to kill it. When Saint George meets it, however, the two become friends and George does not kill the dragon.

The trend of friendly dragons continued in E. Nesbit's 1899 *The Book of Dragons*. Many of Nesbit's dragons are funny and mischievous, while others purr like cats. But by 1937 the fire-breathing terror was back with one of the most famous dragons of children's literature: Smaug.

Smaug is the monstrous dragon that lives below the Lonely Mountain on a pile of treasure in J. R. R. Tolkien's *The Hobbit*. Smaug is sly and supersmart and desires gold above all else. However, he has one weakness: the patch on his belly where a missing scale could allow a well-aimed arrow to penetrate. Tolkien was a professor of literature at Oxford University in England and often gave lectures on the poem *Beowulf* and the story of Fafnir and Sigurd from Viking mythology. These stories gave Tolkien the inspiration for his dangerous fictional dragons—and for dragons that love treasure. Tolkien's books, which include *The Lord of the Rings*, are credited with starting the type of fiction called fantasy. Dragons and

J. R. R. Tolkien

fantasy stories would become steady partners in books throughout the twentieth century and into the twenty-first.

A famous series of dragon fantasy books is the Earthsea Cycle by Ursula K. Le Guin. In 1968's *A Wizard of Earthsea*, the reader is introduced to the fire-breathing dragon Yevaud, who is tired, old, and simply wants to rest. Le Guin's dragons could be powerful and terrible, but also sad and tragic.

Another children's author who showed that dragons weren't necessarily evil was Anne McCaffrey. McCaffrey's Dragonriders of Pern is a series of twenty-four books set in space. On the planet of Pern, humans ride on the backs of dragons to fight an enemy called Thread. The dragons in McCaffrey's books form a deep bond with their riders—like a horse might with its owner. McCaffrey's dragons and heroes are also often female, which marked a change in the male-dominated world of dragons, both in mythology and literature.

The Hungarian Horntail

Dragons in fantasy fiction continued, most famously in author J. K. Rowling's Harry Potter series. Harry Potter introduced ten new types of dragons to the fantasy world, including the Ukrainian Ironbelly and the Hungarian Horntail.

The fire-breathing Horntail is fast and dangerous, much like the dragons in *A Game of Thrones* by George R. R. Martin. *A Game of Thrones* is the first book in the Song of Ice and Fire series, which introduces the reader to firedrake dragons such as Vhagar that can burn down whole fleets of ships, and Syrax, the female dragon ridden by Queen Targaryen.

A Song of Ice and Fire and Harry Potter are both examples of bestselling series that went on to become movies, television programs, and video games. Seeing dragons on-screen gives human beings the chance to experience them up close.

What would the people of ancient Mesopotamia, Egypt, and Greece have thought of these dragons? Would the people of China or Europe in the Middle Ages have recognized the animals on-screen? It seems highly possible, for in movies and on television, almost every type of dragon is represented.

In the 1959 Disney movie *Sleeping Beauty*, the evil fairy Maleficent kidnaps the princess Aurora and then turns into a vengeful European-style firedrake. The 1984 movie *The Neverending Story* introduces a Chinese-style long called Falkor, which helps the hero Atreyu save his world of Fantasia. In the 1996 movie *Dragonheart*, a winged dinosaur-dragon makes friends with the dragon-slaying hero.

The 2021 movie *Raya and the Last Dragon* introduces another helpful dragon that can shape-shift and control water. The How to Train

Your Dragon movie series follows the Viking teenager Hiccup, who decides not to slay but to befriend a dragon. The four feature films, based on the novels by Cressida Cowell, first premiered in 2010. The story was also adapted for television.

Television has had its share of dragons, both friend and foe. There are dragons in Pokémon, *Dragon Ball Z*, and *House of the Dragon*. Many television dragons have also crossed over into video games, such as *Dragon's Dogma, Minecraft, Skylanders*, and *Black Myth*. Such games allow players to fight dragons, ride on dragons' backs, and control dragons as first-person characters on multiplayer platforms.

Perhaps one of the most enduring dragon games is Dungeons & Dragons (D&D), a tabletop role-playing game created in the 1970s. In D&D, a player develops their own character before playing out adventures led by a dungeon master. Gameplay involves fighting a series of dragons, often firedrakes with magical powers. One of the first dragons to feature in D&D was Tiamat, from ancient Mesopotamian myth. In this way, games, television, and movies have kept alive the idea of dragons from our earliest human memory.

CHAPTER 7
Dragons Today

In 2004, American paleontologists reported exciting news from South Dakota. They had found a fossilized skull unlike anything they had seen before. It had a long snout, was covered in spikes and horns, and looked exactly like a dragon skull might look. Had the remains of a dragon finally been found? Was this proof that the creatures once existed? Sadly, no. Paleontologists did agree that the skull looked like a dragon. They even named the species *Dracorex hogwartsia* (say: DRAK-or-ex HOG-wart-see-a), after the school Hogwarts from the Harry Potter books. The creature, however, was not a dragon, but a reptile from the time of the dinosaurs.

This has been the ongoing story of dragons. They originally made up part of the mythology of ancient civilizations. These civilizations probably based dragons on fossils they found in the ground. The remains must have looked amazing to the people who discovered them. They were explained as belonging to dragons. Different cultures viewed dragons differently: In Asia, they were nice; in Europe, they were nasty. But most dragons were large, powerful, and majestic.

Asian dragon

European dragon

The rise of paleontology in the nineteenth century meant scientists became the new dragon hunters. But they also proved that the bones they found did not belong to dragons. Meanwhile, dragons became the central characters of bestselling books. These were dragons with personalities, kind dragons, and dragons that could be ridden like horses.

In the twentieth century, movies, television shows, and video games mixed the many types of dragons together. There were cuddly cartoon dragons; helpful, friendly dragons; and classic vengeful, village-burning dragons. Our idea of dragons has been evolving for thousands of years and has continued into the modern age. Today, we truly live in the golden age of dragons.

Real Dragons

Dragons have been described as flying reptiles that can breathe fire. But today, only birds have the power of flight. That is, except for *Draco* lizards. Southeast Asia's *Draco* lizards have folds of skin that act as wings, which they use to glide from tree to tree. They can glide distances of up to 160 feet, and they look like baby dragons.

But what about animals that can breathe fire, like a dragon? The bombardier beetle comes close. It can squirt a fiery-hot chemical spray from its backside that reaches over 210 degrees! This spray can kill predators that get too close. This is as close as any animal comes to having fiery dragon breath.

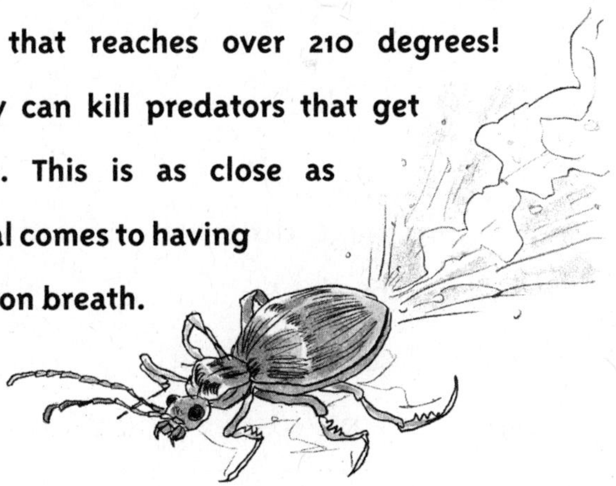

Will we ever find the remains of a real dragon? Anything is possible. Every year, paleontologists discover new dinosaur and reptile species that no one could have dreamed existed. Some look like dragons. In 2021, an Australian pterosaur fossil was discovered with a three-foot-long skull and a twenty-three-foot wingspan. Called

Thapunngaka shawi (say: THAP-un-ga-ka shwi), the flying reptile would have dominated the skies one hundred million years ago and terrorized the animals below. University of Queensland researcher Tim Richards described *Thapunngaka shawi* as "the closest thing we have to a real-life dragon."

In 2024, a team of scientists discovered the remains of a sixteen-foot reptile in China that looked like a long. The reptile, *Dinocephalosaurus orientalis* (say: dino-SEFF-alo-saw-russ ori-ent-aliss), lived 240 million years ago. One scientist described the reptile as a "long and snakelike, mythical Chinese dragon."

These are just the latest dragon-like creatures to be dug up from the planet's distant past. Who knows what else is still buried in the soil, waiting to be discovered? Perhaps one day, we will also find dragons.

Timeline of Dragons

4000 BCE	The first mention of the word *dragon* is written on a Sumerian clay tablet
256 BCE	Roman soldiers report fighting a large dragon near Libya's Bagradas River
206–195 CE	Chinese emperor Liu Bang tells his subjects that he is the son of a dragon
1335	The skull of a dragon is displayed in the town hall of Klagenfurt, Austria
1608	English author Edward Topsell publishes *The History of the Four-Footed Beasts and Serpents*, which includes descriptions of dragons
1836	American professor John Russell writes about the Piasa dragon, once worshipped by the Illini tribe
1882	California's *Gridley Herald* prints an article about a dragon attacking two lumberjacks
1922	American adventurer Roy Chapman Andrews sets out to look for dragon bones in Asia's Gobi Desert
1937	English author J. R. R. Tolkien introduces Smaug the dragon in his children's book *The Hobbit*
1974	Dungeons & Dragons is unveiled
2021	The fossil of the Australian flying reptile *Thapunngaka shawi* is described as the closest thing we have to a real-life dragon

Timeline of the World

4500 BCE	People first settle on the island of Thera, modern-day Santorini, Greece
454 BCE	The Roman public demands reforms to their laws after suffering economic hardship
214 BCE	Construction starts on the Great Wall of China
200 BCE	The city of Tiwanaku is founded on the shores of Lake Titicaca, in modern-day Bolivia
1608 CE	English seafarer and samurai William Adams is presented with titles and land by Shogun Tokugawa Ieyasu of Japan
1836	The Battle of the Alamo between Texas settlers and the Mexican army takes place
1882	Wild West outlaw Jesse James is shot dead by Robert Ford in St. Joseph, Missouri
1937	The Spanish town of Guernica is bombed by the Spanish government and Nazi German Luftwaffe
1959	The revolutionary army of Fidel Castro overthrows the government of Cuba
1970	The Pacific Island of Tonga declares independence from the United Kingdom
2021	The National Aeronautics and Space Administration (NASA) launches the James Webb Space Telescope

Bibliography

***Books for young readers**

Bruce, Scott G. ***The Penguin Book of Dragons***. New York: Penguin Random House, 2021.

Caldwell, Stella A. ***The Magnificent Book of Dragons***. London: Weldon Owen, 2021.

Coleman, J. A. ***The Dictionary of Mythology***. London: Arcturus, 2015.

Mayor, Adrienne. ***The First Fossil Hunters: Dinosaurs, Mammoths, and Myth in Greek and Roman Times***. Princeton: Princeton University Press, 2000.

Mayor, Adrienne. ***Fossil Legends of the First Americans***. Princeton: Princeton University Press, 2023.

*McCall, Gerrie. ***Dragons: Fearsome Monsters from Myths and Fiction***. London: Tangerine Press, 2007.

Niles, Doug. ***Dragons: The Myths, Legends, and Lore***. Avon, MA: Adams Media, 2013.

Shuker, Karl. ***Dragons: A Natural History***. London: Aurum Press, 1995.

Simek, Rudolph. ***Dictionary of Northern Mythology***. Cambridge: D. S. Brewer, 1993.

*Steer, Dugald A. ***Dragonology: The Complete Book of Dragons***. London: The Templar Company, 2003.